Perceptions of writing

Thomas Nelson and Sons Ltd
Nelson House Mayfield Road
Walton-on-Thames Surrey
KT12 5PL UK

51 York Place
Edinburgh
EH1 3JD UK

Thomas Nelson (Hong Kong) Ltd
Toppan Building 10/F
22A Westlands Road
Quarry Bay Hong Kong

Distributed in Australia by

Thomas Nelson Australia
480 La Trobe Street
Melbourne Victoria 3000
and in Sydney, Brisbane, Adelaide and Perth

Nelson Canada
1120 Birchmount Road
Scarborough Ontario
MIK 5G4 Canada

First published by Thomas Nelson and Sons Ltd 1990

Photographs: Chris Ridgers Photography

ISBN 0-17-424122-4
NPN 98765432

Printed in Great Britain by Bell & Bain Ltd, Glasgow

Acknowledgements

Hundreds of teachers and thousands of children have participated in the National Writing Project. They have been supported by many local advisers, members of higher education colleges, parents and others in the community. We cannot name them all, but we would like to acknowledge the commitment of those participants, and trust that these publications represent at least some of their views about classroom practice.

The National Writing Project was set up by the School Curriculum Development Committee. Its three-year Development Phase (1985-1988) directly involved twenty-four local authorities and was funded jointly by the School Curriculum Development Committee and the LEAs. In 1988, the National Curriculum Council took responsibility for the Project's final implementation year.

Central Project Team (Development Phase 1985-1988)

Pam Czerniewska: Director

Eve Bearne
Barbara Grayson
John Richmond
Jeremy Tafler
} Project Officers

Naomi Baker
Anne Hogan
Judy Phillips
} Administrators

Central Project Team (Implementation Phase 1988-1989)

Jeremy Tafler: Director

Georgina Herring
Marie Stacey
} Project Officers

Rosemary Robertson: Administrator

Steering Committee

Andrew Wilkinson: Chair

Dennis Allen
Peter Andrews
Iain Ball
Douglas Barnes
Pat Barrett
Eunice Beaumont
Peter Boulter
Harold Gardiner
Alan Hall
David Halligan
John Johnson
Gulzar Kanji
Keith Kirby
Maggie Maclure
Colin Smith
June Thexton
Jenny Taylor
Mike Torbe
Janet White

Felicity Taylor: NCC Reader

Local Project Co-ordinators

Avon	Richard Bates
Bedfordshire	Mary Heath
Berkshire	Audrey Gregory Barry Pope
Birmingham	Ann Davis Sylvia Winchester
Cheshire	Gill Fox John Huddart
Cleveland	Margaret Meek Joan Sedgewicke
Croydon	Sheila Freeman Iain Weir
Dorset	Barbara Tilbrook Margaret Wallen
Dudley	Chris Morris
Durham	Dot Yoxall
Gwynedd	Len Jones Esyllt Maelor Nia Pierce Davies
Hampshire	Robin Culver Cath Farrow Ann Heslop Roger Mulley
Humberside	Sylvia Emerson
ILEA	Helen Savva
Manchester	Helen Henn Georgina Herring
Mid Glamorgan	Richard Landy
Newcastle	Jay Mawdsley
Rochdale	Frances Clarke Peter Phethean Vivienne Rowcroft
SCEA	Stuart Dyke
Sheffield	Sue Horner
Shropshire	Ned Ratcliffe
Somerset	Vernon Casey Maisie Foster Carole Mason
Staffordshire	Sallyanne Greenwood
Wiltshire	Gill Clarkson Sue Dean Jo Stone

Contents

SIGNPOSTS
SIGNPOSTS

Introduction

Learning in school is not just a question of exposure to instruction in different content areas. Learning is affected by the way in which the curriculum organises information, and the ways in which skills are defined and abilities measured. The nature of our interaction with children significantly affects both their view of learning and their success in the learning process.

Many groups of teachers in the National Writing Project have begun their explorations of writing with such thoughts in mind. How, they have asked, are we presenting the task of writing to children? How has writing been defined by its role in different lessons (for example, something to be done by the end of the lesson; to be done alone and in silence; to be handed in to the teacher) and by the way in which we evaluate it? How have children's views about the nature and purpose of writing been affected by reminders about spelling or deadlines, for example?

In this pack we have included a number of teachers' explorations of children's writing experiences and their perceptions of those experiences. We have also set out some means of learning more about writing from the child's point of view — questionnaires; diaries; writers' portraits — and some follow-up ideas.

Finding out what pupils think and say about writing is only a starting point. It has to lead to major decisions about our criteria for children's writing. For example, do we want them to value presentation more than content? What changes (if any) could we make to our strategies if we find that pupils object to collaborative writing? What activities could we initiate for pupils who can name only two kinds of writing? Discussion of these crucial questions has led to the many classroom activities recorded in the other Theme Packs. This collection reflects experiences which were, for many teachers, the catalyst for changing the writing curriculum.

Consultative Group

Pam Czerniewska
Gill Fox
Sue Horner

Further in-service resources for examining children's (and teachers') views of themselves as writers and of the writing curriculum can be found in *Making Changes* (Nelson).

SOUTH KOREA
MALAYSIA
FINLAND
BELGIUM
ARGENTINA
PERU
SIMPLE

1 Children's attitudes to writing

The National Writing Project has examined and documented many children's perceptions of writing; examples have been drawn from all age groups. Teachers have used questionnaires, structured discussions, interviews and writing tasks to elicit children's views.

Thoughts from young writers

The first two accounts — one from Sheffield and one from Dorset — typify children's perceptions about writing.

What do children (aged between four and seventeen) think about writing and writers? Do their views change as they grow older?

'I can write big things.'

Jane (aged 5)

'Writers make their writing neat and someone types it out and it gets sold as in storybooks.'

Kevin (aged 8)

'Writing is to keep contact and to communicate for pleasure, to send messages, to keep in touch with your family or friend who you have not seen for a while.'

Zoe (aged 13)

Team members from the Writing at the Transition Project in Sheffield were interested to see whether these responses were typical. Teachers were asked to elicit their pupils' views about writing and writers. These were collected and analysed to see whether any patterns emerged.

The questions asked were the same in all the schools, and the teachers agreed to take reasonable care that the answers were not discussed. It was important that the results represented individual children's opinions.

These were the questions:

- Who writes?
- What does a writer do?
- What do they write?
- What happens to their writing?
- Are you a writer?
- When do you write?
- What happens to your writing?
- Can you draw a writer?

The children who took part in the survey were from nine classes in seven schools, ranging from a nursery school to a sixth form centre. All the classes were mixed ability groups. Some of the teachers had previously been involved with the Writing Project, but others had not. As the work was carried out early in the school year, the teachers and children were fairly new to each other. The teachers were interested in finding out what their pupils' perceptions were at this stage.

Certain general patterns emerged in the replies:

Four- to six-year-olds

- Writers are people known to the children.
- Writing happens at home, and has various purposes.
- Younger children are confident in their ability as writers.
- As children become aware of the demands of letter formation and writing conventions, they become less confident writers.

Eight- to eleven-year-olds

- Writing happens on a grand scale — stories, films, scripts for publication.
- Writing is public, for a wider, often unknown audience.
- The more people who read the writing, the more valuable the writing is.
- Writing seems to have some connection with learning.

Twelve- to thirteen-year-olds

- A range of forms of writing is clearly identified.
- Each form is seen to be related to purpose and to the writer's role; for example, *'Doctors write prescriptions'*.
- Personal and domestic uses of writing are emphasised.

Seventeen-year-olds

- Writing gives access to other people's experience — past or present — and this is important.
- Writing (and more widely, the media) informs opinions.
- Entertainment and escapism form a significant purpose for writing.
- Writing is permanent, not transient.

Looking specifically at issues of who writes what, the nursery class teacher anticipated that her children would find the concept of a writer abstract and beyond their experience. In fact, the four- to six-year-olds responded by defining a writer in terms of their own experience:

Sometimes for letters...for invitations. I write for my Mum and in my number book. I send messages to people.

Jane (aged 5)

stories things to post
diary shopping list
typing business dad

Hayley (aged 6)

Between the ages of six and ten, children began to perceive an author behind a piece of writing, particularly if it was a story:

1. A woter wotes Books
2. we wate storys
3. my mum wites
4. A woter writes things
5. A water writes storys.
6 A water writes Lettes
7 A waters writing some teme gets pubilst

Paul (aged 8)

Authors were clearly the most important part of the process for Richard. He also identified a range of purposes for writing which are important for the reader. Phrases such as *'writing to be read'* and *'for others to read'* were most commonly found in responses from this age group.

Authors write quite ogten. parents write notes to their greinds or realatives. Children write to do their work at School. A writer thinks what he is going to do before he does it. A writer could write storys for Adults and children. writers could write letters they could do work. and lots og other things. Authors writing Sometimes gets published Children's writing gets put up on the wall in School.

Richard (aged 12)

A new feature appeared in the responses given by lower Secondary pupils — writing as a means of expressing feelings.

Writing can be for many different reasons like these... to be read, to express your feelings, to tell people things to say what you feel and to express other peoples feelings as well as your own. Writing is a type of comunication.

Tim (aged 11)

For sixth formers, the emphasis was on raising awareness and informing judgement. Reading other people's writing gave them a form of vicarious experience.

> The writer enable us to see the world through the eyes of others By sharing their feelings and various subjects we have the power to broaden our minds and increase our opinions. Writers have a wealth of ideas to share with us all be it through novels, newspapers or magazines - they all have great importance in society.
>
> . . .

Louise (aged 17)

In terms of who writers are, four- to six-year-olds most commonly identified family and friends as writers.

Eight- to nine-year-olds also identified writers in their immediate circle, but there was a growing consciousness of authorship and public writing.

WRITER.S

My MUM is a good WRITER.S
and my DAD is a good WRITER.S
THEY WRITERS a BOk peIPOL
ik is good Because They WRITER.S
good.

James (aged 8)

Many of the pictures drawn by these pupils showed writers surrounded by the formal paraphernalia of an office: desk, typewriter, desk light, piles of papers, and so on.

Matthew (aged 8)

In the ten- to thirteen-year-old age range, the children specified physical features and other personal qualities which writers should have. These were very varied.

Some people dont just write some are very active and do a lot of Sport Or others just relax at home thinking about their books and getting fat

I think that writers should be middle aged and they should be calm

Other qualities mentioned were patience and *'being sensible'*, and it was certainly important for writers to *'not have bad tempers'*. There seemed to be a suspicion amongst these pupils that writing was somehow not quite a 'normal' activity, although writers might otherwise be ordinary people.

A writer does not only write he/she does the things normal people do

This tendency to eccentricity was linked with being *'clever'* and *'creative'*.

I think A Writer is supposed to be a wierdo but I write family stories and I am not wierd

There was evidence of stereotyping in the children's pictures; a majority of the writers depicted were wearing glasses and were male. This tendency was nevertheless balanced by the idea that anyone can be a writer, regardless of personal qualities.

Anyone who wants to write can, unless they haven't got any paper.

Throughout the sample, teachers were seldom identified as writers. Only three children between the ages of four and eleven made this connection. When teachers were mentioned by the Secondary children it was in the context of the idea that everyone is a writer, and that writing may have specified functions related to work.

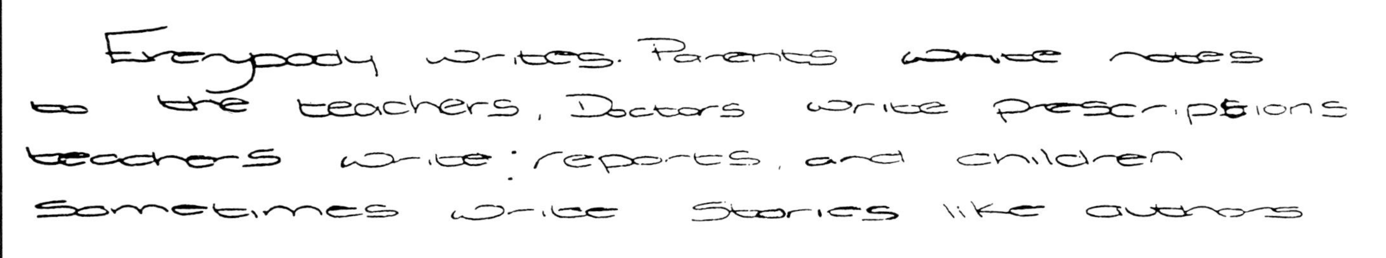
Everybody writes. Parents write notes to the teachers, Doctors write prescriptions teachers write: reports, and children Sometimes write Stories like authors

The idea of teacher as writer was conspicuously absent when the nursery teacher talked to her children, and this was viewed with concern by the staff. Since then, the children have been given opportunities to see the teacher in this role, and the head teacher has recently involved the children in her yearly task of sending out letters to parents about the Harvest Festival.

Throughout the age range, the majority of children did see themselves as writers. The youngest children exhibited confidence and excitement about writing in their responses . . .

'I type, I write as well.'

Alana (aged 4)

. . . but as they grow older this mood is undermined by an awareness of constraints and difficulties. The comment below is in answer to the question *'Are you a writer?'*

No, but Ican do letters. I'm hopeless at words.

Older children answered this question in terms of how a writer is defined, rather than in terms of personal capability.

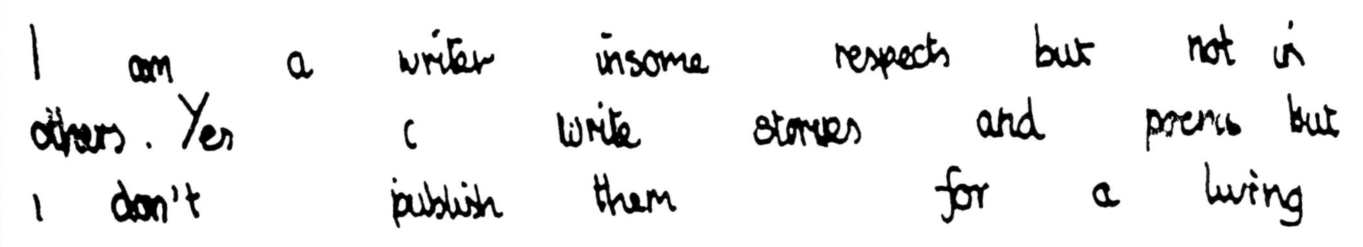
I am a writer insome respects but not in others. Yes I write stories and poems but I don't publish them for a living

It seems that children's views of writers and writing are influenced by their experiences at school. Teachers found that asking these questions helped them to discover their pupils' views, and then to build on and extend the ideas.

Kath Stallard, Sheffield Writing Project

Writing about writing

A mixed ability class of nine-year-olds in Dorset were asked to write about writing. A few were able to grapple with the difficult concept of what writing is:

'I think writing is a skill and there is no other subject like it.'

'Writing is like a lot of scribbles and each scribble means something.'

'I see writing as a description of things. Writing is a bit like pictures but the pictures are being described for you.'

They seemed confident about their understanding of why we write, and showed awareness of a wide range of motives:

'I think we write because it is another way of communicating with one another.'

'I like writing when bored because it gives you something to do.'

'I like to write because you can write to people you like.'

'People write so they can get a job. We write to help us learn and get a job so we can make money.'

'Sometimes we write so the teacher knows what we are thinking.'

'People who have got pensions write because it will give them something to do before they die.'

'What you write is up to you if you are at home, and if you are at school it is up to the teacher what you write about.'

Like many professional writers, children can be rather neurotic about the physical conditions necessary for writing:

'To be a very good writer you have to have a very smooth hand and a very sharp pencil or a nice pen. I started writing because for one thing I like writing italic and I've got a very nice smooth pen. When people write books they do it on a typewriter which is cheating but there's not a law saying you can't use a typewriter.'

'The problem is your arms ache and get tired and you have to stop work and when it doesn't ache you start work again.'

'Pens have a secret way of running out when you are writing with them. Mine has done that lots of times.'

They were very sure, and rather perceptive, about the qualities which a good writer must have:

'To be a good writer you have to think. You have to.'

'You have to love writing to be a writer and you must be quite clever to have all the ideas in your head to come out or to write on to a piece of paper so you could just go on.'

'If you want to write well you have to do quite a lot.'

'That is what to do to become a good writer (a) determined (b) like writing (c) like reading.'

'The thing you need mostly for writing is that you should concentrate.'

'You should not start talking. Then you will not be a good writer.'

One quality they were definite about was technical accuracy:

'To be a good writer you have to be a good speller.'

'You have to do your best when you are writing and you have to put capital letters and full stops so that you won't have to do them again and make your writing messy by crossing out or having to write a word on top of another, because that makes your work look worse than it is.'

'To be a good writer you have to be neat, careful and quite quick.'

Clearly there is teacher influence at work here. Some is quite explicit:

'Writing is for you to be able to know more words and to do neater writing. Writing shows your teacher how you are progressing.'

'When I do a piece of writing with the rough draft first you check all the mistakes and then you think you have put them all right but the teacher finds a mistake that you couldn't find.'

Even those who appeared to have a sense of audience for their writing should probably have substituted 'teacher' for 'people':

'When you write a piece of writing you should do it neatly so people can read it, not messily so that people cannot read it.'

A few, however, seemed genuinely to be aware of an audience 'out there', even if the motives of the first one were a little mixed:

'I like writing because you might get a housepoint if it is very good. I like writing because it can be up on the wall so other people can see it and I will see theirs.'

'Writing is fun especially when you write to people. The people that you send it to probably enjoy reading it as much as we enjoyed writing it.'

Many of the group considered writers to be members of an élite which they were not likely to join:

'When you write a book it has to be sold in the shop but our writing has not.'

'Not many people want to be writers so whoever does will have no trouble at all getting on.'

'It takes a long time to be perfect.'

Others seemed to have gained a more realistic concept of what it means to be a professional writer:

'To be a good writer you need to make lots of attempts before you finally succeed in getting a good piece of work into the shops. Some artists, writers the world will never know because they have never got their writings or pictures into shops to sell.'

'Writers read a lot themselves and they get ideas from different books sometimes.'

Encouragingly, many children contradicted their earlier comments and showed that, for some of the time at least, they did think of themselves as writers:

'I like writing very much. I have liked it ever since I knew how to write.'

'There is no limit to what you can write. Some people write pages and pages and some people write only a few. It doesn't matter how you write even if it's about Porky Pig it doesn't stop you from writing about it.'

'Writing is different to everything else in the world. When I am writing I think about my writing not what is going on around me.'

'I have often felt proud of my writing.'

Children who had decided that writing was not for them seemed at least to know why:

'I do not do much writing because I do not enjoy it, but you can do a lot with writing. Sometimes it can be very important anyway most of the time I'm out.'

'I would not make a good writer because (a) I have not much patience (b) I do not like writing. Writing is not my favourite subject.'

And finally, some words of encouragement for us all:

'But you have to write a lot to become famous. I don't know anybody who has become famous but don't think you can't because you can . . . Writing is easy when you know how.'

Margaret Wallen, Dorset Writing Project Co-ordinator

Follow-up ideas 1

Reactions to the children's responses in surveys such as these were, predictably, mixed. Positive attitudes towards writing, expressed by many children, were welcomed; they clearly derive enjoyment from many writing tasks. Alongside the pleasure, though, there were some less welcome views which demanded teachers' attention. The following summary indicates some of the main concerns teachers identified and the actions they initiated.

Concerns	*Action*
Children often judge the success of their writing by its neatness, spelling and punctuation rather than by the message it conveys.	Many teachers have tried to take the focus away from neatness and accuracy by encouraging children to understand the writing process. Classroom ideas have included: — showing other writers' drafts including revisions to style and content — talking about difficulties such as how to get ideas; how to decide on the best way of conveying a message; how to evaluate neatness — encouraging children to invent spellings or to leave gaps at first draft stage, thus promoting the idea that such aspects are not important until a later stage of production
Children often have difficulty in talking about their own development as writers except in very broad terms.	Children have been encouraged to keep personal folders of their 'best' pieces of writing and to reflect on their achievements and concerns over a period of time. By keeping records of all drafts for a particular piece of work, they can also reflect on progress made within the production of a text.
Children see writers as people who publish books (usually stories); writing is thus thought about in terms of end products.	Greater emphasis has been placed on the role of writing for learning. For example, many teachers have introduced planning stages whereby children jot down and talk about ideas, questions and tentative thoughts before they study a particular topic. (For more about this idea, see *Writing and Learning*.)
Writing is often seen as a school activity whose primary purpose is to show teachers what has been learned.	More attention has been given to the different audiences and purposes available for writing. In particular, teachers have found readers for children's work in other classes and other schools, thus reducing the teacher's role as the sole evaluator of effective writing. (See also *Audiences for Writing* and *Writing Partnerships (1): home, school and community*.)
Writing is seen as an individual activity; ideas for writing are rarely discussed and outcomes rarely shared with others.	Teachers have encouraged collaborative writing activities in which children discuss their ideas, write together and use each other as readers/responders to their work. (See also *Responding to and Assessing Writing*.)
Writing, talking and reading are not always clearly associated with each other.	Writing activities have been promoted as preliminaries to many non-written outcomes (storyboard writing for films; scripts for radio broadcasts). Young writers have been encouraged to see themselves as critical readers of their own and others' writing.

Resources 1: Questions and discussions

Questionnaires can be a way into exploring children's perceptions. The first example is intended only as a 'consciousness raiser' to show pupils that they are writers, that writing exists outside school, and that there are many everyday uses for writing. It can be used by individuals or in a small group. It provides a starting point for discussion about different kinds of writing and their uses.

Ways of writing

What sorts of writing do you do at home?	In which lessons do you write at school?
1 ______	1 ______
2 ______	2 ______
3 ______	3 ______
4 ______	4 ______
5 ______	5 ______
6 ______	6 ______
7 ______	7 ______
8 ______	8 ______

What sorts of writing do you do in those lessons? (Stories, poems, one-sentence answers, factual reports.)

1 ______	5 ______
2 ______	6 ______
3 ______	7 ______
4 ______	8 ______

The next questionnaire was devised for Middle school children. In the school where it was originally used, teachers had been perturbed to find that their children viewed writing as essentially a secret, solitary activity. They went on to develop ways in which pupils could collaborate and share their writing as part of the drafting process.

Think about all the writing you have done. Which kinds of writing do you enjoy most?

What do you find the hardest thing about writing?

Think about the best pieces of writing you have done.
What made them good?

Are there times when you find writing boring? When are they?

Do you like other children to read your writing and comment on it?

Do you find that it helps to talk about your writing before you write? Why?

In what ways has your writing improved?

What can your teachers do to help you write better?

What changes do you make when you rewrite your work?

Teachers of younger children have found it useful to ask them to look through the writing they have done during the last week, selecting the most pleasing piece and the most disappointing piece. Teachers in Rochdale developed a questionnaire which allowed quite detailed analysis of children's criteria for pleasing/disappointing writing and of the process of its production.

Writing Questionnaire

School ....

Pupil .... Age .... Male/Female ....

1 Details of work chosen

	Pleasing piece	Disappointing piece
Type of writing		
Length of writing		
Illustrations		

2 a) Pleasing piece – Significant qualities

Question: Why does this one please you?
(Number these factors 1-7 in the order in which the child refers to them)

	Number	Comments
Length of piece		
Neatness		
Technical accuracy		
Content		
Type of writing		
Grade/mark/teacher comment		
Other (Please specify)		

b) Disappointing piece – Significant qualities

Question: Why does this one disappoint you?
(Number these factors 1-7 in the order in which the child refers to them)

	Number	Comments
Brevity		
Untidiness		
Number of errors		
Content		
Type of writing		
Grade/mark/teacher comment		
Other (Please specify)		

3 a) Pleasing piece – Pre-writing activities

Question: What did you do before you started writing?

	Number	Comments
Nothing		
Can't remember		
Read		
Listened		
Watched television		
Other (Please specify)		

b) Disappointing piece – Pre-writing activities

Question: What did you do before you started writing?

	Number	Comments
Nothing		
Can't remember		
Read		
Listened		
Watched television		
Other (Please specify)		

4 The writing process

	Pleasing piece	Disappointing piece
i) Did you write it more than once?	Yes/No	Yes/No
ii) Did you ask the teacher to help while you were writing?	Yes/No	Yes/No
iii) Did you help anyone else with their writing?	Yes/No	Yes/No
iv) Did any of the class help you?	Yes/No	Yes/No

5 Post-writing – Pleasing piece

i) Who did you write it for? ....

ii) Who else do you think might want to read it? ....
....

iii) What did you want to do when you finished it?

	Number	Comments
Read it out		
Show the teacher		
Read a friend's writing		
Do a drawing		
Go on to something else		
Other (Please specify)		

iv) What could we do with it now?

	Number	Comments
Put it on display		
Tape record it		
Take it home		
Other (Please specify)		

Whatever the nature of the questionnaire — general or specific, open-ended or requiring specific answers — it can help pupils to clarify some of their thoughts about writing. It can also provide starting points for teachers to examine their own thinking and teaching, so that they can plan either to reinforce or to change their pupils' perceptions of writing.

Alternatively, it is possible simply to ask children to write under the general heading of *'My writing'* or *'When I write'*. A variation on this is to ask pupils to write letters of advice to younger children on the subject of writing, telling them what they need to know in order to succeed in writing during the coming year. The aim is to assess what pupils perceive to be the most important aspects of writing.

Myself as a writer

When my Big sister Angela started school I was only 2yrs old I was a little bit jealous because I wanted to write. But when I first started School I noticed that I was not the only one who could not write. My first piece of writing was about my family. we used to have to write all in pencil, and I found it easier to write in pen.

My mum gave most of her time to me so that I would beable to be a good writer then and now. In Junior school the teachers used to write on my work 'Gina tidy up your work" I used to tell my mum and she said 'well then you must try" ...

Another way of discovering pupils' perceptions of writing is through teacher-led discussion in small groups. Although it is important that the conversation should develop naturally so that pupils can pick up points from each other, agree and disagree, and explain their thoughts and feelings, it is helpful to raise specific questions to initiate discussion. The following questions, organised under four headings, have proved useful:

1 *What they do and what they like*

What different kinds of writing do you do?
How are these different from each other?

Do you like writing? What kinds of writing do you prefer? Why? What kinds of writing do you not like? Why? Do you like to be told what to write about or do you prefer a free choice?

Who do you do your writing for?

Do you do any writing at home? Is it different from what you do in school? How? Is this more/less enjoyable than the writing you do in school? Why?

2 *What's important and what they're good at*

Is being able to write important? Why? Are certain types of writing more important/useful than others? Which? Why?

What are you like as a writer? What are you good at?
What are you not good at?

What makes a piece of writing good? Suppose someone was writing a story, or was writing about something that had happened to him/her; what would (s)he have to do to make it a good piece of writing?

3 *How they do it*

(Either in general terms or with reference to a particular piece of writing)

Where do you get your ideas from? Once you know what you're going to write about, how do you set about it? Do you discuss your ideas with someone? Do you jot down your ideas/make a plan/start writing? Do you write in rough first/several times/write in best straight away? If you write in rough, what kinds of change do you make? How might your final version differ from the first?

4 *What response they'd like to get*

What do you like (dislike) to happen to your writing? Do you like to have it displayed/read out/kept in a folder? Why? How do you like the teacher to mark your work? What sort of comments are helpful/unhelpful; pleasant/unpleasant? What do you not like?

One teacher who used this means of exploring her children's perceptions of writing found — amongst other things — some revealing attitudes towards story writing. In response to the question *'What do you think makes a good story?'* many of the children were able to pinpoint features that contribute to a good piece of story writing. They were aware of the need for an interesting plot that captures the audience's attention at the beginning and sustains their attention throughout. They mentioned the inclusion of dramatic incidents with believable characters, and description and realism where necessary. However, only a small group of the most confident writers could attempt to explain how this could be achieved.

In spite of their enthusiasm for story writing and their confidence that this was an easy type of writing, many of their comments suggested that they suspended all critical faculties whilst writing and adopted a kind of 'anything goes' attitude. Looking with fresh eyes at some of their most recent stories, the teacher felt that there was a gap between their knowledge of what made a good story and their own stories, which were often rambling and undisciplined, containing flat characters and little or no description, and which terminated abruptly when the writer grew tired or bored.

This teacher went on to find ways of helping her children develop their writing so as to include in their own stories those features which they appreciated as central to a good piece of story writing.

6 children took size
3 children took size
2 children took size
2 children took size
Teacher Washi
Ladybird Books

2 A lesson in language learning

For adults, writing usually has clear purposes and functions. Writing may mean jotting down items on a shopping list as a reminder, exploring ideas in an essay for a course of study, persuading in a letter of complaint, or musing on events in a diary. In each case the writer knows why the writing is necessary, what it should achieve, who will read the writing and what might happen to it in the end. For each piece of writing these factors are different. How does this compare with the writing done by pupils in school? Will the purposes and functions of writing be as clear and as varied?

Teachers may feel that they have various reasons for asking pupils to write, which might include: ensuring that pupils have notes for revision, checking that pupils can perform certain operations, allowing pupils to express their ideas and develop them, encouraging pupils to write imaginatively, testing the accuracy of the writing . . . and more. Many of these purposes are specialised and relevant to the particular content of education, unlike ordinary, everyday purposes. Although pupils' experience is, eventually, extensive, their understanding of what they are asked to do is necessarily different from that of their teachers, not least as a consequence of the unequal distribution of power and influence in classrooms.

In Sheffield and Mid Glamorgan, teachers have looked a little more closely at these issues to see exactly what kinds of writing are found inside and outside school, and how these uses are perceived by different people.

Writing inside school . . .

Teachers and pupils in Sheffield and other local authorities have found it useful to keep diaries, recording all the writing done during a short period of time. Teachers noted what they had set, why they had set it and any comments they wished to make. Pupils noted what they had done, why they thought it had been set and what they thought about it.

These examples from different Sheffield schools compare the teachers' and pupils' perceptions of the purposes of particular tasks.

Task: Answer ten questions about a History programme 'How we used to live'

Teacher's purposes	*Pupil's purposes*
To build up historical knowledge	Pupils 1 and 2 To teach us history
	Pupils 3 and 4 To help us do sentences

In this instance, pupils 1 and 2 have a similar understanding to that of the teacher: this is a History lesson. From the evidence of pupils 3 and 4, though, it seems likely that, when setting the task, the teacher had said something like *'Don't forget the punctuation.'* If the pupils thought the writing was a punctuation exercise, they may have failed to grasp the historical significance of what they had seen.

Task: To substitute alternatives for the word *'said'* in ten given sentences

Teacher's purposes	*Pupil's purposes*
To learn to use words rather than *'said'* – to extend vocabulary and to help with story writing	Pupil 1 To learn other words for *'said'* Pupil 2 To learn to understand things like how to use different words instead of *'said'* when people are speaking in stories Pupil 3 To improve our vocabulary, spelling and punctuation Pupil 4 To use our imagination

For this highly specific task, pupils 1 and 2 are in tune with the teacher, and pupil 2 has even appreciated the intention to transfer the point of the exercise into their stories. Pupils 3 and 4 seem to have written what they assume are the generalised intentions behind any English or language work — technical accuracy or use of the imagination. It is not clear from their perceptions of purpose whether they are likely to achieve what the teacher wanted or not, since they have not engaged with the particular point of this task.

Task: A rough draft: Why we have rules; different sorts of rules (codes, instructions, law); the Country Code

Teacher's purposes	*Pupil's purposes*
To follow the Country Code in preparation for a week's visit to Mayfield (an outdoor centre); to be aware of rules in life generally (why we have them and why we need to abide by them)	Pupil 1 Because we are going to Mayfield Pupil 2 I think it was set so we know about the Country Code and to take care of it and make it a nice place to live in Pupil 3 I think it was set so we know the rules of our country and it is because of rules it is a lot better country

In this task, the teacher's purposes were more numerous and were at different levels of relevance and abstraction. The pupils have interpreted the teacher in different ways, but all of them see what they are doing as relevant and even worthwhile. It is likely that these pupils will achieve at least a measure of success in this task since they have identified reasons for doing it which make sense to them, either in the short term (for the impending visit) or more generally.

If the pupils' perceptions of the reasons for doing something are very different from those of the teacher, the nature and quality of their learning must be affected. For instance, if the full extent of the teacher's intentions is not appreciated by the pupils, their learning is likely to be partial or even incidental, and, at worst, the pupils' perceptions may subvert the teacher's intentions to such a degree that none of the educational aspirations are fulfilled.

In the experience of teachers in the National Writing Project, pupils work more effectively when they know why they are writing, for whom the writing is intended, and the criteria by which the writing will be judged. Writing is one element of the experience of pupils in schools. For effective learning to take place, learners need to know where this particular activity fits into the general pattern, what they are expected to achieve, and why it is considered valuable to them. Better still, learners may be able to see other equally valid reasons for activities, and may progress beyond the teacher's expectations because they can see for themselves where particular activities may take them.

If there is agreement between teachers and pupils about the reasons for doing a particular task, pupils may be persuaded that education is a reasonable enterprise. This, in turn, may crucially alter the basis of the relationship between the teacher and the taught, since there are grounds for discussion about not only what is to be done but also the reasons for doing it.

If learners need contexts and purposes which are meaningful, it is important that teachers provide opportunities in which purposes may be made explicit. This is a process of exploring, explaining and agreeing, so that the ground is clearly laid and pupils know the teacher's reasons for setting a piece of work. They also need to know that their views and purposes have been taken into account. Differing but compatible purposes which are clearly recognised are preferable to implicit assumptions about what is going on. It is important that discussion of the purposes of writing is not confined to an explanation by the teacher; several purposes, perhaps at different levels, may be inevitable and even desirable. Pupils, if given encouragement, are likely to be able to relate what they are doing to their own interests and if they see personal relevance in a writing task, they will probably fulfil the teacher's intentions too.

It is essential, then, that teachers find time to make explicit their reasons for setting particular pieces of work, and try to discover how pupils view the tasks and their own performance of them.

In the first instance, this is likely to include specific occasions when issues about writers and writing, about pupils' views of themselves as writers and learners, and about teachers' views of purposes and criteria for success in writing are raised. These occasions are significant as they legitimise the whole area as one which is important in the classroom, and they also allow agreed aims and interests to be recognised and developed and common ground to be established. As this sort of debate becomes commonplace, it seems likely to become a natural part of classroom work. If pupils are keeping logs regularly, they may include comments on the writing they do. If pupils discuss their work regularly with their peers, they are likely to be involved in explaining why they have written as they have. If the teacher regularly offers choices to pupils, they are likely to develop rationales for their decisions.

Sue Horner, Sheffield Writing Project Co-ordinator

. . . And outside school

One of the questions that our Mid Glamorgan group investigated was *'How much correlation is there between the writing that is done in school and the writing that is done in the world outside?'* We were aware that we really didn't have very much information. So I suggested to the twenty members of my fourth year Office Studies class that we undertake a survey to see what differences, if any, there were. The pupils were very enthusiastic, and decided that we were interested not only in the writing that was done as part of people's jobs, but also in the other writing that they might do as part of their daily lives. Essentially, we wanted to see whether or not the different types of school writing were relevant to the writing students would do after leaving school.

Each pupil was given a small notebook and was asked to keep a daily record of all the writing that they had done, on one side of a double page. Each pupil enlisted someone outside school — perhaps a parent, relative or friend — and on the opposite side of the page recorded all the writing done during the course of each day by this 'volunteer'.

After two weeks we began to collate the information, using only information from complete logs. We drew up a list of writing activities which had been undertaken (a) by both pupils and adults, (b) by pupils only, and (c) by adults only. Obviously, the sample was rather small and somewhat random, but the adults included a bank clerk, a secretary, a receptionist, a personnel manager, an engineer, a teacher, houseworkers and several people who were unwaged.

We were surprised and intrigued by some of the findings. Although a number of the writing activities were done both inside and outside school, there were marked differences in their relative proportions. Essays don't seem to figure strongly among out-of-school writing activities, and nobody 'out there' seems to be answering questions from worksheets! On the other hand, real-life writing jobs such as reports and surveys don't appear to be well represented in the school's writing curriculum. I've listed the raw data below. In many cases, it seems to speak for itself.

Since we did the survey, I've been thinking about ways in which this work could be developed on a larger scale, using more accurate data. I intend to make a survey of this kind the basis of a project for the GCSE Office Studies course.

Activities undertaken by both pupils and adults

By pupils		*By adults*	
Charts/diagrams	27	Charts/diagrams	2
Birthday cards	12	Birthday cards	4
Personal letters	11	Personal letters	14
Essays	33	Essays	3
Business letters	1	Business letters	12
Informal notes	3	Informal notes	6
Log book entries	105	Log book entries	20
Notes	61	Notes	6
Form filling	3	Form filling	33
Bingo	7	Bingo	45
Football pools	1	Football pools	9
Telephone messages	2	Telephone messages	9
Marked exercises	20	Marked exercises	1
Crossword	22	Crossword	39
Competitions/puzzles	4	Competitions/puzzles	9
Appointments	2	Appointments	9
Shopping lists	1	Shopping lists	13
Paying-in slips	1	Paying-in slips	4
Typing	12	Typing	14
Mail-order documents	3	Mail-order documents	2

Activities undertaken by one group only

By pupils only		*By adults only*	
Doodling	2	Cheques	17
Worksheets	45	Envelopes	10
Answering questions	58	Pension books	4
Writing on the board	1	Accounts	14
Labelling	1	Betting slips	4
Signing name	3	Scoring sheets	10
		Telephone notes	9
		Pay queries	3
		Reports	6
		Surveys	3
		Clock-cards	2
		Invoices	14
		Memos	2
		References	4
		Bank communications	13

Anne Greenaway, Lewis Girls' School, Ystrad Mynach, Mid Glamorgan

(See 'Writing in school and at work' in the Theme Pack *Writing Partnerships 2: school, community and the workplace.*)

Follow-up ideas 2

Reviews of writing and the writing curriculum have revealed a number of features that have prompted teachers to consider different learning approaches within their schools.

Ned Ratcliffe, Shropshire Writing Project Co-ordinator, summarises the findings from a number of surveys and identifies some ideas that have been developed in response.

Thinking about writing

The following points emerged from the surveys carried out by Shropshire teachers:

- A great deal of the writing performed in school comes at the end of a sequence of activities — as a summing up of what has been learned or is supposed to have been learned.
- Much of the writing is brief:

  sentence completion

  questions to be briefly answered

  structured worksheets with limited space for writing
- Much of the writing consists of the simple transfer of information from one place to another, often by copying.

Such experience does not make the most of the potential of writing in enabling and supporting learning. It ignores the possibilities that writing offers:

- to organise old and new experiences
- to capture emerging ideas
- to reflect on experience
- to work out problems
- to try things out
- to 'think' on paper
- to communicate meaning

Activities in which writing appears to contribute considerably to a pupil's learning include:

Making use of writing throughout the learning process

(brainstorming; hypothesising; pooling ideas; note-making; discussing interim findings; asking own questions; using planning devices — topic webs, splash charts, storyboards, branching diagrams)

Using writing in an incidental way to help produce non-writing outcomes

(class or group discussion; debates; role-play/simulations; maps; designs; graphs; diagrams; working models; spoken presentations with support materials; radio/ television programmes; slide-tape sequences)

Offering opportunities to use a wide range of formats

(brochures; manuals; poems; logs; lists; reviews; posters; questions; instructions; stories; play scripts; labels/captions/signs; advertisements; catalogues; diaries; letters; cartoons; accounts; newspaper articles; journals; postcards; notes; accounts of experiments; circulars; notices)

Using writing for a wide range of purposes

(recording; planning; persuading/arguing; explaining; hypothesising/predicting/ speculating; reorganising; describing; instructing; empathising; reflecting;

exploring/investigating; questioning; advising; summarising; generalising; reasoning; narrating)

Writing for a variety of audiences . . .

. . . within the classroom

(wall displays; class newspapers; class anthologies; reports/talks; other groups in the class)

. . . within the school

(younger classes; assemblies; school magazines; booklets/brochures; surveys/reports)

. . . in other schools

(letter exchanges; individual/class stories/booklets for younger children; presentation of research)

. . . and beyond

(publishing in the local community; newspapers; radio; guides/booklets; parish magazines; newsletters for parents/families)

The following example shows how such considerations about writing can assist pupils' learning.

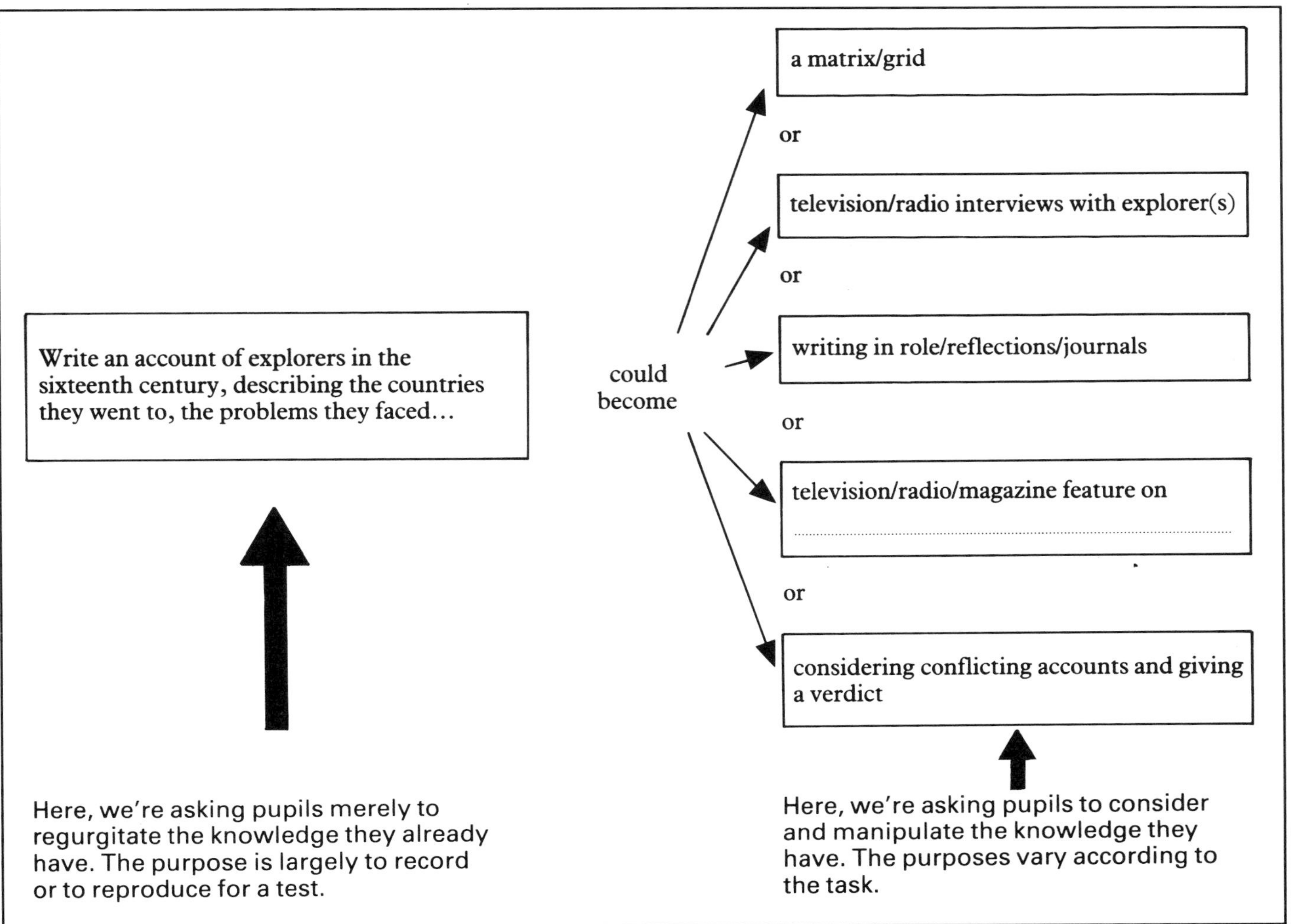

Ned Ratcliffe, Shropshire Writing Project Co-ordinator

Resources 2: Records of writing and writers

Writing journals or logs can be useful as a means of focusing on pupils' perceptions of the process of writing, while at the same time helping them to develop a sense of themselves as writers.

The journals can be completely unstructured, so that pupils can reflect on their writing in whatever manner they choose, or they can be like the one in the example that follows. Each child was given a 'log book', containing a guidance sheet followed by printed sheets for their own use.

Where these have been used, teachers have commented not only on the benefits for themselves (in terms of insights into their pupils' attitudes and approaches to writing), but also on the benefits their pupils have derived from comparing their reflections with those of their friends. Such discussion has opened up the process of writing to pupils, and encouraged them to find ways of helping themselves and each other to develop their writing.

What I was asked to do

Give some brief details here about what your teacher wanted you to do, for example: *We were given a list of ten titles, and asked to choose one and then write a story that would fit the title. I chose 'Catastrophe'.*

Reflections on my writing

Here you can write about anything that is to do with your writing. Depending on what happened, you might like to comment on:

— whether you were keen to begin
— how you got your ideas
— how you set about putting these ideas on paper
— what went well with your writing
— what difficulties you encountered and how you dealt with these
— what help you got
— if you had a plan, how far you kept to this plan
— whether you wrote the piece straight out or whether you worked in draft form
— if you did the latter, what sort of changes you made
— how enjoyable or unpleasant you found the writing task
— how satisfied you were with what you had written

These are only suggestions. You may write as little or as much as you wish, about anything of interest and/or importance to you in connection with your writing.

If you wish to write more, continue on the back of this sheet.

The teacher's comments and my response to them

Briefly note the teacher's response to your writing here – perhaps give the mark and the comments you received. What were your thoughts about what was said?

A variation on this is the following activity.

Pupils are asked to make notes in answer to some of the questions below, just before they start a particular piece of writing. When they have finished the writing, they can discuss or write down any observations they have about their original answers and what they actually did. Focusing pupils' attention on the process involved in doing a piece of writing opens up the whole area of what writers do and what stages a piece of writing goes through.

What do you think this piece of writing will be about?

What sort of writing will it be?

Will you enjoy doing it?

How long do you think your piece of writing will be?

How long will it take you to do it?

Where will you get your ideas from?

What sort of planning will you do?

Is there anything that you or your teacher could do that might help you with your piece of writing?

Will you read your work through when you've done it?

Will you make any changes to it?

Will you be pleased with it when you've finished it?

Would you like anyone else to see it as well as your teacher?

What will your teacher put on your work?

To look specifically at the question of whose writing it really is and where the ideas come from, pupils can be given the following sheet and asked to complete it in relation to specific pieces of writing. This might be restricted to writing in one particular subject area, or used to reflect on the whole curriculum. This is a useful tool for evaluating what is happening in the classroom and indicating what changes, if any, would be valuable in particular areas of the curriculum.

Is/was the writing...			
... all in the teacher's words?	... mostly in the teacher's words?	... mostly in your own words?	...all in your own words?
Are/were the ideas...			
... from your teacher?	... mostly from your teacher?	... mostly your own?	... all your own?
Do/did you...			
...not like it much and want to get it over as quickly as possible?	... think it was all right but feel glad when it was finished?	... think it was good and get involved in what you were doing?	... think it was great and get really involved in what you were doing?

The following idea focuses on pupils' and teachers' perceptions of the purposes for writing, but concentrates on a specific piece of writing. Pupils are given a number of statements, and asked to list them in order of importance as reasons for the piece of writing they are in the process of doing or have just completed. This exercise is useful in finding out whether there is a match or a mismatch between pupil and teacher perceptions of a given task, at the same time raising pupils' consciousness in terms of what they are doing and highlighting reasons for writing of which they might previously have been unaware.

— to get better at spelling, punctuation and writing sentences
— to make better use of your imagination
— to learn to work with others
— to help you to sort out your ideas and plan stories
— to enjoy hearing and writing stories
— to show the teacher how much you have understood
— to show yourself how much you have understood

A cross-curricular approach to exploring children's perceptions of writing may be made through the use of diaries. Pupils keep a record of the writing they do (and teachers the writing they set) over a one- or two-week period.

For example, teachers in Sheffield used a diary approach in which pupils were asked to record:

- the date and the time of the writing
- the nature of the writing task
- their perceptions of why it was set
- the nature of the readership
- their comments

Records of this kind can demonstrate the match or mismatch between the purposes stated by the teacher and the pupils' perceptions of them, and can provide opportunities for pupils to comment on the writing they do.

In the Project, teachers have responded to children's perceptions of writing concerning purpose, audience or the nature of the task. For example, they have found ways of making their intentions clearer to their pupils, or of helping them to distinguish between the various functions that writing can fulfil and the various forms it can take. In one case, staff broadened the range of audiences available for their pupils' writing. In another, a school moved away from a writing diet which relied too heavily on the completion of worksheets. The nature of the follow-up work is, of course, determined by what is revealed in the studies.

3 Pupils as writers

When writing activities are surveyed, when pupils' views of writing are elicited, when perceptions of writing — why it happens in school and how it is judged — are discussed, a picture gradually emerges. It becomes clear that the learner not only actively constructs the writing task, but also constructs a view of himself/herself as a writer.

This is a vital perspective on the learner. It is easy to forget that when reading incidental remarks at the bottom of a piece of paper or a routine instruction, the child is working out what kind of writer (s)he is. Children are learning from and negotiating with those around them to work out their role in the literacy culture.

Portraits of young writers

Teachers at Bankfield High School in Cheshire tried to learn more about children's views of themselves as writers.

We wanted to devise an activity that would combine all the advantages and possibilities of supportive group discussion and lead to pupils drawing up some kind of portrait of themselves as writers, using a minimum of writing. Such an activity, we realised, needed a structure that would help generate ideas, promote purposeful discussion and also provide support for the teacher.

Our initial idea involved dividing the class (first year Juniors) into small friendship groups of between four and six pupils. We then gave each pupil a sheet of A3 paper with a figure of a pupil in the centre, and two A4 sheets on which were printed a variety of statements about writing. The idea was that pupils would discuss these statements, select and cut out those that applied to themselves, and stick them on to the large sheet alongside the figure. (We tried to get printed stick-on labels but they were far too expensive!)

The pupils were invited to choose as many or as few as they wanted, and to add comments to any of the statements if they wished. The important point was that they chose only those statements with which they agreed. Those they rejected were collected in an envelope, with the intention to consider the reasons for their rejection. However, we never found the time or the energy to delve into the envelopes! During and after the selection process, the class teacher could choose to intervene, to join in with groups, or to wait and discuss the completed portraits with individuals in later lessons.

In the first session the response was very positive, with pupils busily engaged in discussing the statements and sticking them on to the 'big sheets' to build up their portraits. Unfortunately, however, they were not able to finish the work during that double lesson. When the activity was resumed after a break of several days, they seemed less committed and had to be encouraged to finish.

Looking over the completed sheets afterwards, we were pleased to confirm that it was possible to build up a picture of how a pupil saw himself/herself as a writer, by noting which statements (s)he had chosen. (Interestingly, we had noticed during the lessons that some individuals altered their initial perceptions as a result of positive intervention from their peers.) It was also possible — by drawing all the information together — to build up a composite picture of the attitude to writing of the class as a whole. All these findings were encouraging since they suggested that the basic idea was sound, but at the same time, problems were all too apparent.

First, because pupils were able to present the statements in any order on the A3 sheets, it was difficult to assimilate the information quickly. Secondly, it was obvious that certain terms such as *'share'* and, more importantly, *'writing'*, were not always understood in the sense in which we were using them. *'I am good at writing'* meant *'I am good at handwriting'* to some children, possibly because we had failed to explain things sufficiently. Thirdly, and again this was probably the result of inadequate explanation, pupils did not always realise that in some cases 'blanket' statements were available. For example, one pupil cut out and stuck on all the *'I like . . .'* statements, not realising that *'I like doing all kinds of writing'* had been provided.

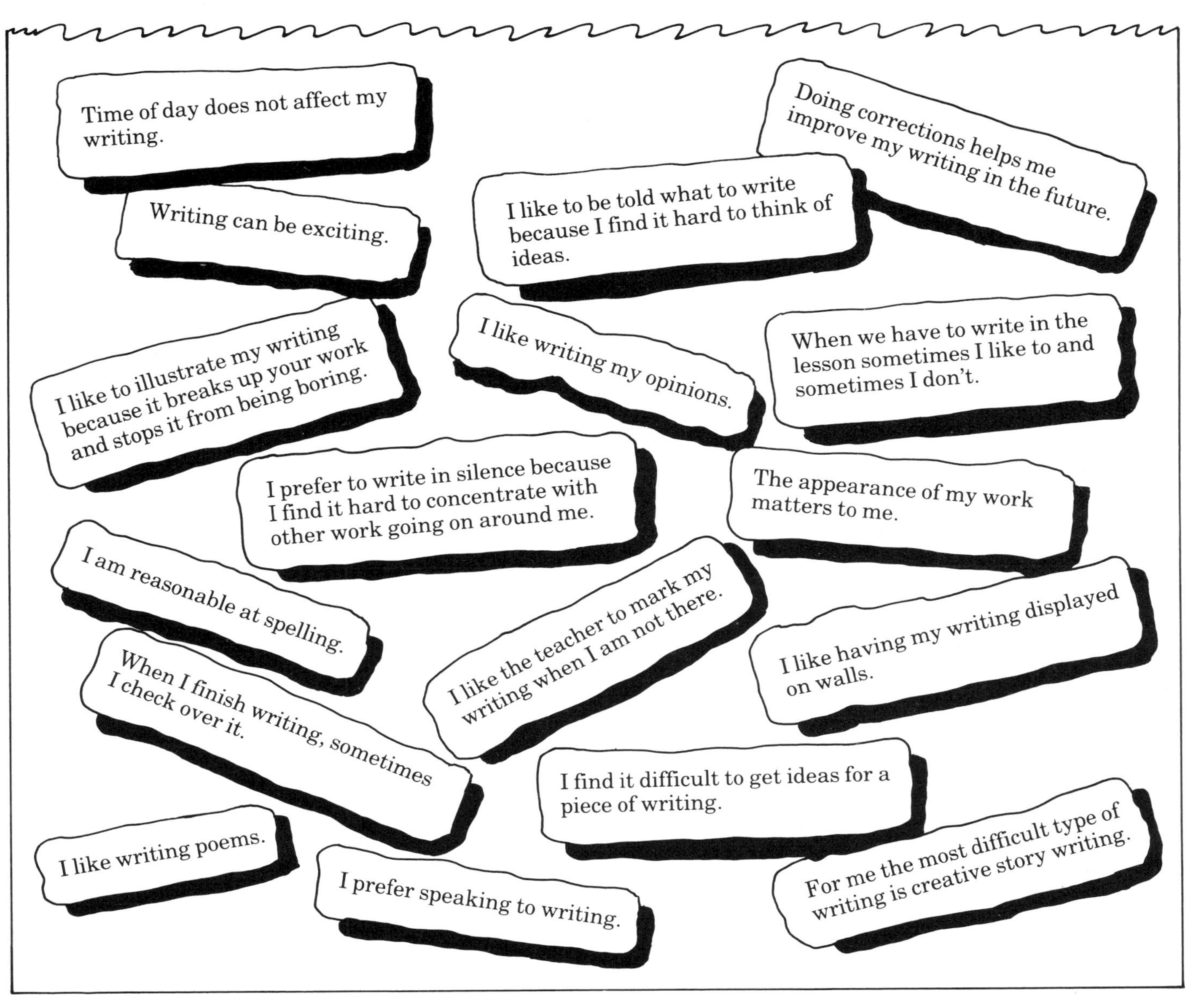

Although we now knew a great deal about our pupils' attitudes and approaches to writing we were unclear as to what our next step should be. We could see that there were implications for our teaching of writing in the long term, but we wanted to do something immediate and specific that would increase the pupils' awareness of what is involved in writing. We tried to draw their attention to trends in their selected statements and to discuss the reasons behind some of the selections, but this didn't work too well — probably because the novelty of the exercise had worn off.

When we tried the activity with the next class, we refined it in an attempt to improve matters. We divided the statements into five sections — for example, the writing process; likes/dislikes. Statements relating to each section were printed on paper of a particular colour, so that when we came to look at an individual's selection we would be able to build up a picture more easily. In the lesson, we divided the class into five groups and imported some extra help so that each group had an adult to work with. We selected one of the sections and discussed the statements in detail so that everyone understood the activity. When the discussion was completed, the pupils selected their statements and added their comments. This procedure was followed for each section of statements.

Despite the presence of a few individuals who failed to become totally involved, the activity was much more successful this time. The completed portraits were more informative, as the terms were better understood, the choices were more knowledgeably made and explanatory comments were provided. During the discussions (in which ideas were fruitfully exchanged and explained), it seemed that the pupils were thinking more deeply than usual about writing. Unfortunately, we did not record the discussion, and this was undoubtedly a lost opportunity.

Because the portraits were more informative this time, drawing together all the information enabled us to build up a more revealing composite picture of the attitude of the whole class. We thought we would be able to use this to help our pupils develop as writers. For example, although virtually every pupil believed that writing was important, all but one (who said *'it helps you work things out when you're working'*) stated that this was because you need it to *'get a job'*. This suggested an understandably utilitarian attitude, but also that we have more to do in communicating to children our reasons for valuing writing.

Other interesting evidence, which we are considering when planning future teaching, emerged from the portraits. For example, we now know more about: pupils' preferences in writing; the degree of difficulty they assign to certain types of writing; the variety of conditions they consider helpful; their feelings about what should happen to their writing and what kind of response it should have.

We were conscious of the need to build an accessible record of pupils' perceptions which they could return to, review and, perhaps, rework. We still wanted to find more objective proof that the process of selecting statements actually enhanced their awareness of themselves as writers and deepened their perceptions of writing. We had no doubts in our own minds, but it is always comforting to see subjective feelings confirmed by objective findings!

Therefore, we decided to make use of the English department's self-assessment English profile which had been developed and trialled for all pupils to complete at six-monthly intervals. We wanted to study the profiles to see whether they would confirm our earlier findings — that statement selecting helped pupils to arrive at a better understanding of writing in general and their own writing in particular.

Again we focused on first year new-intake children. One class completed their profiles after going through the statement-selecting and portrait-building process. Another completed the profile without selecting statements first.

Once more, the whole class participated enthusiastically in the discussion and selection process. It was again obvious that pupils found considerable pleasure and interest in building up their own portraits. All the positive features we had observed in earlier attempts were again apparent, with the discussion groups providing many examples of insight and increased understanding of the issues. This time, too, we encouraged the pupils to devote a particular area of the A3 sheet to each type of label, thus helping us to draw conclusions more easily.

The difference between the two classes in their approach to the profiles was very clear, though it must be pointed out that the non-statement-selecting class was given no support when filling in the profiles. Their (supply) teacher was asked to give advice only to individuals who made a point of asking for it.

When we compared the two sets of profiles, we were struck by the fact that the statement-selecting group had made lengthier and more thoughtful comments. These pupils commented in more detail on a greater variety of aspects, and virtually all — even the weakest among them — gave reasons for their observations. The following comments are typical:

'I like writing stories as long as they are enjoyable. I like stories to be enjoyable and exciting. I sometimes have good ideas but I have a lot of trouble writing them down on paper. Most of my ideas come from books I have read and programmes I have watched on television.'

Fay

'I like writing informal letters especially to my Auntie Elsie because I always find lots of things to say to her in the letter. And no matter what, she always wrights one back. With lots of exciting things in it.'

Yvonne

'I find writing poetry difficult because when I read some one elses theres are always better than mine and I can never get mine to rythm and it sounds arfull and when I ask them doese it sound all right they just say yes for the sake of it so they dont afened me but it doesen't help me atal.'

Anne-Marie

It seemed that members of the statement-selecting group were distinguishing 'writing' from 'handwriting'; separate comments were made about handwriting and how they felt that it affected their writing generally. With the non-statement-selecting group, most referred vaguely to writing and it was impossible to tell whether or not they were aware of a distinction; for some, though, 'writing' definitely meant 'handwriting', and they praised or condemned themselves according to how they viewed their calligraphic skills.

The reflective nature of these responses was not confined to the part of the profile concerned with writing; it extended into other areas of English. We feel confident that the more sophisticated and reflective approach of this group was a direct result of their preliminary work on the statements.

Although the activity has been modified along the way, we feel that it still has some basic flaws which make it cumbersome to administer and review. For example, we would like to try using an A4 booklet instead of the sheet, dealing with particular aspects of writing one at a time. This would give pupils more time for discussion and reflection before compiling and completing. When engaged in the statement-selecting, the pupils will enjoy even more opportunities for personalising their document. Some have already started to introduce photographs in place of the drawing, and a booklet would allow a series of different images. Also, a booklet would be much more useful as a reference document and as a pointer for future teaching.

Jim Foley, Bankfield High School, Widnes, Cheshire,
and Gill Fox, Cheshire Writing Project Co-ordinator

Resources 3: Statements and profiles

Working with sets of statements can be a particularly useful way of helping children to think about their writing. The following warm-up exercise is one of many approaches. Groups of children are given a list of provocative statements:

Boys are better writers than girls.
Stories are easy to write.
Writing is the most important thing we do in school.
Writing poems is fun.
It's important to write neatly.
Silence is best for writing.
You have to be clever to write well.
Teachers should correct all mistakes.
It's silly to write about things which can't really happen.
Starting a piece of writing is the hardest thing.
The longer the writing, the better it is.
Talking to a friend helps you to write.
Bad spelling spoils writing.
The best stories have happy endings.
It's easier to write about things you can see.
You need to make mistakes in order to learn to write.

Each group is also given a large sheet of paper divided into three columns headed: *'Agree', 'Don't agree'* and *'Don't know'*. The group has to decide where each statement should go, cut it out and paste it on.

This has proved to be a useful activity. Teachers have been surprised by the level of discussion, and have found that this helps to prepare children for the issues to be raised in more detail later. A variation on this activity is to give groups of children pairs of statements on cards, for example:

A good piece of writing could contain punctuation errors.  A good piece of writing contains no punctuation errors.

Either you are a good writer or you are not. 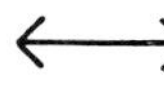 Anyone can become a good writer.

Each pair of cards is discussed, the group retaining the statement they agree with and rejecting the other. The chosen statements can be pasted on to a large sheet of paper and compared with the choices made by other groups. Again, important issues are raised as part of the process.

The next example is more straightforward in that pupils are given a writing profile booklet with headed pages in which, in response to questions, they reflect on themselves as writers. The areas covered are likely to include:

- attitudes to different types of writing
- the way in which writing is tackled
- how pupils assess themselves as writers

. . . depending on what the teacher wishes to draw pupils' attention to. Follow-up work — as with the 'portraits' — will depend on the nature of the responses elicited. The following example is from a Writing Profile booklet currently being used with fourth and fifth year Secondary pupils.

When doing a piece of writing

Some pupils prefer to write in draft first. Do you? Yes/No ....

When (or if) you are drafting, what kinds of change do you usually make?

....

....

....

How do you feel about drafting? Do you enjoy or dislike it, think it useful or a waste of time – or what?

....

....

....

Strengths and weaknesses

When talking about their strengths and weaknesses as writers, pupils often refer to: the ideas they have for writing; the way they organise these ideas; the way they express them; spelling and punctuation. They also reflect on the various types of writing they are required to do and consider whether they are better at some types than others.

What do you think are your strengths?

....

....

....

Are there weaknesses too? What are they?

....

....

....

Endnote

Where do I go from here?

Some of the activities suggested in this pack encourage pupils to reflect generally on writing — its purposes and forms — both within school and beyond. Other activities have been designed to help pupils to consider their writing diet in school, and to think about their personal strengths and weaknesses in writing. In other cases, a single piece of writing is used as a basis for asking pupils to examine the purposes and processes of writing, and the responses they receive.

Having considered their pupils' views, teachers in the Project have identified priorities for action, which include: introducing a greater variety of writing forms; writing for a wider range of audiences; linking writing more closely to learning; helping pupils to have more choice in their writing and placing greater emphasis on the processes of writing.

Eliciting pupils' comments produces feedback for teachers which may result in changes to the writing curriculum. Ideas for doing this may be found in the other packs.

Continuing consultation

Many teachers have found that their pupils had a very limited view of the writing they did in school. The 'hidden' curriculum dominated their ideas. To help pupils to make the most of opportunities, there are several steps which may be taken:

1. When setting up work, explain:

   'I want you to do this because. . .'

2. Having accustomed pupils to the idea that there are reasons for doing the task, ask:

   'I want you to do this because . . .

   What do you think?'

3. Having accustomed pupils to the idea that they should discuss the reasons, ask:

   'What do you think we should do to build on the work we have done so far?'

4. Having accustomed pupils to the idea that they should plan together with the teacher, ask:

   'Did we achieve what we set out to do?' and

   'What else did we learn?'

In these ways, a recognition of pupils' perceptions may be built into classroom practice on a regular basis.

One of the most significant opportunities offered by such questions is that, jointly, pupils and teachers may recognise achievement and identify progress.

Towards independence

Learning is much more likely to be effective when the learner understands what is to be learned, why, and what the ultimate goals may be. Asking pupils to reflect on these acknowledges that individuals have a variety of ways of working. Understanding the range and knowing when to work in any particular way is essential if learners are to become autonomous and independent, making informed choices on the basis of experience and advice. Part of our job as teachers is to provide this range of experiences and to offer relevant advice, but this alone is not enough. In order to ensure the effective use of the experiences and the advice, their usefulness must be made explicit and the subject of discussion. Subsequent choices are thus informed by a proper evaluation of the alternatives — the basis for independence.

We need to continue to acknowledge the range of perceptions in our classrooms; to acknowledge that the teacher's values are not the only ones and that learners may take away a variety of possibilities from our lessons. Giving our pupils continuing access to the decisions of the classroom can only improve our chances of providing a relevant and valued curriculum.

Sue Horner, Sheffield Writing Project Co-ordinator